explaining...
AUTISM

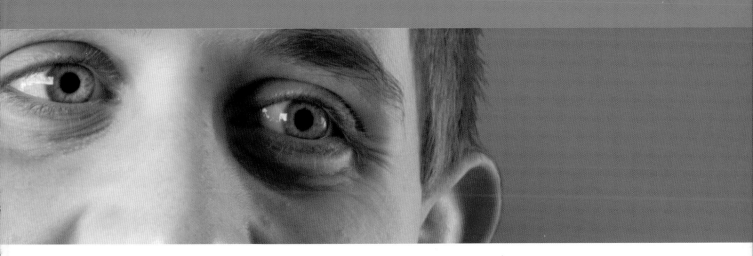

W
FRANKLIN WATTS
LONDON·SYDNEY

ROBERT SNEDDEN

First published in 2008 by
Franklin Watts
338 Euston Road
London NW1 3BH

Franklin Watts Australia
Level 17/207 Kent Street
Sydney NSW 2000

ISBN 978 0 7496 8252 1

Dewey classification number: 618.92'85882

A CIP catalogue record for this publication is available from the British Library.

Planning and production by Discovery Books Limited
Managing Editor: Laura Durman
Editor: Annabel Savery
Designer: Keith Williams
Picture research: Rachel Tisdale
Consultant: Dr John Lawson, Senior Research Associate, Autism Research Centre, Cambridge; Senior Lecturer in Psychology, Oxford Brookes University.

Printed in China

Franklin Watts is a division of Hachette Children's Books, an Hachette Livre Company.
www.hachettelivre.co.uk

Photo acknowledgements: Corbis: pp. 35 (Ed Kashi), 36 (Kat Wade/San Francisco Chronicle); Discovery Picture Library: pp. 21 (Chris Fairclough), 22 (Chris Fairclough), 25 (Chris Fairclough); Essex Autistic Society/www.essexautistic.org.uk: p. 37; Getty Images: pp. 8 (David Young-Wolff), 18 (Hulton Archive), 38 (Karen Kasmauski); istockphoto.com: pp. 13 (Jason Stitt), 19 (Eileen Hart), 28 (Deanna Quinton Larson); John Birdsall/www.JohnBirdsall.co.uk: front cover top and bottom right, pp. 9, 15, 20, 26, 27, 29, 31; Johns Hopkins Medical Institutions: p. 10; National Autistic Society: p. 16; National Fragile X Association: p. 39; Southern Illinois University Carbondale: front cover bottom left & p. 32 (Steve Buhman); Science Photo Library: pp. 23 (Professors P. M. Motta & F. M. Magliocca), 30 (Annabella Bluesky)

Source credits: We would like to thank the following for their contribution:
Autism Speaks www.autismspeaks.org.uk/case_studies.html (p. 17); The team at the Autism Centre for Education and Research (ACER) at the University of Birmingham for NES NHS Scotland www.nes.scot.nhs.uk/asd/casestudies/natasha.htm http://www.nes.scot.nhs.uk/asd/casestudies/david.htm (p. 29, p. 37); Lola Fisher and The National Autistic Society http://www.nas.org.uk/nas/jsp/polopoly.jsp?d=125&a=10377; 'Make schools make sense for me' by Beth Reid and Amanda Batten, published by The National Autistic Society, 2006; Joshua Muggleton http://mugsy.org/joshua; http://www.templegrandin.com/

Please note the case studies in this book are either true life stories or based on true life stories.

The pictures in the book feature a mixture of adults and children with and without autism. Some of the photographs feature models, and it should not be implied that they have autism.

Contents

8 What is autism?

10 Autism: a brief history

12 The rise of autism

14 The autistic spectrum

16 The signs of autism

18 Autism and inheritance

20 The triggers of autism

22 Autism and the body

24 Autism and mental health

26 Can autism be treated?

28 Living with autism

30 Autism and families

32 Autism and school

34 Asperger syndrome

36 Autism and adulthood

38 The future for autism

40 Glossary

42 Further information

44 Index

What is autism?

By some estimates as many as one in every hundred schoolchildren in the UK have a condition called autism. In the United States the rate is thought to be about one in 175 children. Boys are roughly four times more likely than girls to be autistic. Up until the middle of the twentieth century, this condition, that affects so many people and their families, did not even have a name.

Autism is not a disease

An important thing to understand about autism is that it is not a disease. You cannot 'catch' autism. People with autism have a brain that has developed differently. They do not see the world in the same way that a person without autism sees it. This means that a person with autism may have difficulty communicating with other people and forming relationships with them.

A person with autism does not look any different from a person without it. This can make autism difficult to recognise. Dealing with autism can be a challenge. Living with a person with autism can be tricky for the other members of the household because people with autism do not understand the needs of others and often cannot express what their own needs are.

▼ *A child who has autism looks no different from any other child.*

Usually it is the parents who are the first to spot the changes that signal that a child is different. When a child who had appeared to be developing normally suddenly becomes quiet and withdrawn, the effect on the rest of the family can be devastating.

The autistic spectrum

Autism can be hard to diagnose because it covers a wide range of conditions. This is called the autistic spectrum and we shall look at this in more detail on pages 14-15. Autism does not come in one form and its severity can vary from one person to another. People with what is known as high-functioning autism can be very bright, with normal or above average learning skills, whereas a person with low-functioning autism is likely to have learning difficulties as well.

▲ *Being in a crowd of people at a concert is great fun for most people, but for someone with autism it can be noisy, confusing and upsetting.*

DESCRIBING AUTISM

A person with autism described the condition like this:

'Reality to an autistic person is a confusing mass of events, people, places, sounds and sights. There seem to be no clear boundaries, order or meaning to anything. A large part of my life is spent just trying to work out the pattern behind everything.'

Autism: a brief history

Autism has probably always been around, but it is only in the last 60 years or so that it has been recognised and described as a medical condition.

Leo Kanner

In 1943, Dr Leo Kanner of Johns Hopkins University in Baltimore, USA, published the results of a study of eleven children carried out over five years. Most of these children had withdrawn from social interaction by the age of two. Describing one of the children, Kanner wrote:

'He seems to be self-satisfied. He has no apparent affection when petted. He does not observe the fact that anyone comes or goes, and never seems glad to see his father or mother or any playmate. He seems almost to draw into his shell and live within himself.'

Kanner used the word 'autism' (from the Greek word 'auto', meaning 'self') to describe these children. He believed strongly that there was a biological reason for their condition. As the condition appeared so early on in life he did not think there could be an outside cause for it, he believed they were born without social instinct. Several years later people began to suggest that autism was the result of bad parenting, for example by mothers, referred to as 'refrigerator mothers', who were too cold and uncaring towards their children. Kanner himself was swept along with this tide of thinking. Understandably this idea, which has now been rejected, caused considerable distress to the parents of children with autism.

◄ *Doctor Leo Kanner, (1894 - 1981), who did much to increase our understanding of the condition that he named autism.*

THE WILD BOY OF AVEYRON

In 1799, the Frenchman Jean Itard wrote the first detailed description of a child we now believe to have had autism. This so-called 'wild boy' was captured by hunters in a mountainous region of France. At the time of his capture, he was naked and filthy, unable to speak and so lacking in any social skills that many people thought he must have been raised by animals. It may be that he was orphaned at a young age or abandoned by his parents. Itard began to work with the boy, naming him Victor. Over the next few years Victor made some progress – he wore clothes and slept in a bed, but he never learned to talk. He remained autistic throughout his life.

Hans Asperger

In 1944, Austrian doctor Hans Asperger published the first description of the condition, Asperger syndrome, that was named after him. He studied four boys in whom he observed abilities and behaviour that he called 'autistic psychopathy' (from 'autism' – self, and 'psychopathy' – meaning a disease of the personality). The boys had difficulty forming friendships, were apt to be clumsy and were likely to become single-mindedly involved in what they were doing. Asperger called them 'little professors' because of the detail they would go into in describing favourite topics. As a child, Asperger himself was said to have shown some of the symptoms of the condition he described. You can read more about Asperger syndrome on pages 34-35.

The rise of autism

Since the 1980s there appears to have been a dramatic rise in the number of children being diagnosed as having autism. The United States Education Department, for example, reported that the number of autistic students had risen by 544 per cent between 1992 and 2000. What could be the reasons for this increase?

A change in diagnosis

As mentioned, autism covers such a wide range of symptoms that it is difficult to diagnose. In fact, it was not until around the mid–1990s that doctors came to agree on how it should be diagnosed. So part of the reason for the increase could be greater awareness among doctors of the signs of autism. Children who might once have been classed as having learning difficulties may now be diagnosed with autism, for example.

Levelling out?

In 2003, a study of 567 children in north-east London who were born between 1979 and 1998 and who had been diagnosed as having an autistic spectrum disorder (ASD) was published. This study showed that, following an apparent rise in the

▼ *There has been a dramatic rise in the number of cases of autism being diagnosed in recent years. The reasons for this are as yet uncertain.*

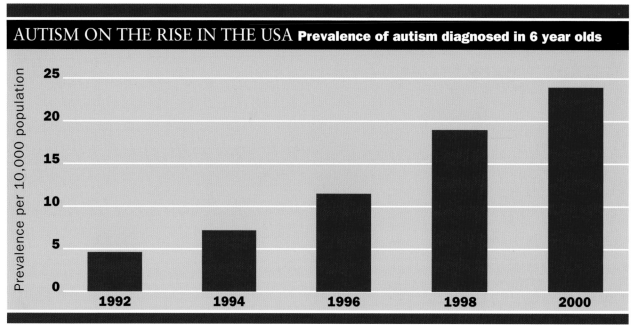

AUTISM ON THE RISE IN THE USA **Prevalence of autism diagnosed in 6 year olds**

Source: American Academy of Pediatrics

number of ASDs from 1979 to 1992, the condition reached a peak of 2.6 cases per 1000 children between 1992 and 1996. Lead investigator, Brent Taylor, professor of community child health at Royal Free and University College Medical School, London, said that the levelling off suggested that the increase in autism was not a real rise, but instead reflected the changes in diagnosis and a greater willingness by people to accept the condition. More recent studies have shown there to be 10 cases in every 1000 children.

Other ideas

Other researchers dispute Taylor's conclusions and are convinced that the rise in reported cases of autism is a very real one that cannot be explained away by changes in diagnosis. The emphasis, they say, should be in trying to determine the causes of this increase. Investigators are looking into a

number of possibilities but nothing conclusive has yet been found. Pesticides, vaccinations, plastics in bottles, processed food and other forms of pollution are all being examined. These environmental factors might not actually be the cause of autism, but some believe they may make the symptoms more pronounced (see pages 20-21).

MOBILE PHONES AND AUTISM

There have been attempts by some researchers to link the rise in autism with the increased use of mobile phones and wireless networks. It is claimed that the radiation from these gadgets disrupts normal brain cell function. Other researchers say that the level of radiation is so low that it could not cause any real damage and that phones are perfectly safe to use.

▶ *It has been suggested that mobile phones might be involved in the increase of autism, but there is no real evidence to support this.*

The autistic spectrum

'If you have met one person with autism, you have met one person with autism.' This is something that people who work with people with autism and in autism research might say. What it means is that people with autism are quite unlike one another – each is a unique individual with unique needs.

Autistic spectrum disorder is a term that is used to describe a group of disorders. These include classic autism and similar, related conditions such as Asperger syndrome. It is because the degree of autism can vary so markedly from one person to another that autism is referred to as a spectrum disorder.

The range of autism

People with autism face a range of difficulties – from those who are less able with lower than average intelligence, to those at the higher end of the spectrum who may have higher than average intelligence.

▼ *Autism is described as a 'spectrum' disorder because it covers a broad range of conditions.*

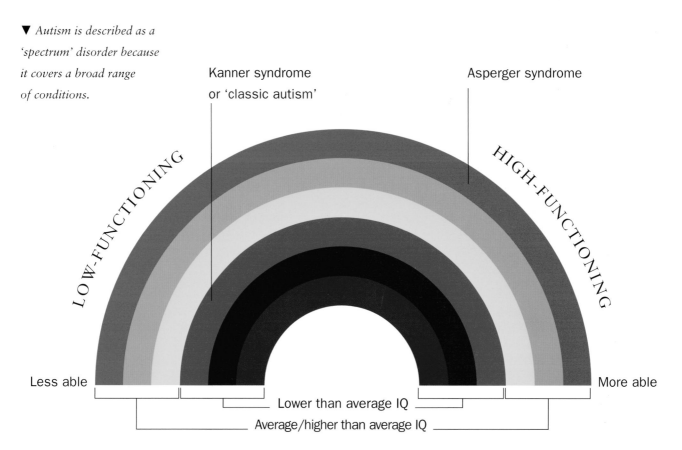

Kanner syndrome or 'classic autism'

Asperger syndrome

LOW-FUNCTIONING

HIGH-FUNCTIONING

Less able

More able

Lower than average IQ

Average/higher than average IQ

People who are at the low-functioning end of the autistic spectrum are said to show Kanner syndrome as they fit the description of the children studied by Kanner (see page 11). This is also sometimes described as 'classic autism'.

At the other end of the spectrum are high-functioning people, whose symptoms are similar to those described by Asperger. Those people at the high end of the spectrum still have difficulties with language and communication, but these difficulties are not nearly as marked as those shown by people at the low end of the spectrum.

Similar conditions

Rett syndrome is a rare condition. It is not an ASD, but some of the symptoms are similar, though often more severe. Unlike autism, Rett syndrome only

▲ *Joseph is 22 and has classic autism. He has a great interest in books and loves reading.*

affects females. One in around 10,000 to 15,000 girls will have the condition. The child develops normally at first, then sometime between six and eighteen months they begin to show symptoms which may be similar to those of a child with autism.

Childhood disintegrative disorder (CDD) has similarities with autism and Rett syndrome. It is an extremely rare but devastating condition. Fewer than 1 in 50,000 children will develop CDD. The child develops normally up to the age of three or four and then suddenly loses his or her abilities, including language and social skills, control over their movements and control of their bowels and bladder.

The signs of autism

There is no medical test that can be used to diagnose autism. There is no blood test, for example, that can be used to tell if a person has autism or not. The doctor must look for three main signs in diagnosing an autistic spectrum disorder. Together these signs are known as the 'triad of impairments'.

These signs can only be looked for once the child has reached a certain stage of development. When the child's development is checked at 18 months, a doctor screening for autism will ask the parents a series of questions. They may use the Checklist for Autism in Toddlers (CHAT). The answers to these questions allow the doctor to assess whether or not the child may have autism.

Dr Lorna Wing

Dr Lorna Wing is well known as a researcher in the field of autism. It was Dr Wing who coined the term 'autistic spectrum disorders' and who introduced the idea of the triad of impairments (see page 17). She studied a number of children in the Camberwell area of London in 1979 and observed that:

'...all the children with social impairments had repetitive stereotyped behaviour and almost all had absence or abnormalities of language and symbolic activities. Thus the study showed a marked tendency for these problems to occur together.'

Dr Wing, in other words, was seeing children who would perform a few simple actions over and over again, who seemed unable to communicate with others through speech or writing and who had no understanding of other peoples' thoughts and feelings.

▼ *Dr Lorna Wing is one of the world's foremost researchers into the causes and characteristics of autism.*

The triad of impairments

1: Social problems The person with autism will find it difficult to interact with other people socially and be unable to chat with others. Some talk at length about their special interests and do not give any space to others to join in. They will seem not to know what behaviour is appropriate in different circumstances. They will not readily form friendships with other people.

2: Communication problems The person with autism can have difficulties in understanding and interpreting other people's feelings. They do not pick up on facial expression, body language or tone of voice so they do not pick up on mood, such as knowing if the person talking to them is happy, angry or sad. Some have problems with grammar and vocabulary but others have fluent speech – their difficulty lies in the way they use their speech.

3: Lack of imagination Some people with autism will not engage in games or activities that involve the use of imagination and may prefer repetitive activities. Some copy the imaginative activities of other children, but without any real understanding. Others invent their own imaginary worlds, which may be very elaborate, but are not shared with others.

These are not hard and fast definitions. Each person will have different levels of difficulties on each component of the triad. This is what makes it so difficult to understand the needs of a person with autism and makes each one unique.

▶ *Dr Wing introduced the idea of the 'triad of impairments' – three key factors in diagnosing autism.*

TIM'S MOTHER'S STORY

'At 10 months Tim would push his wooden trolley filled with his favourite trains and tractors making the exact noises you would expect to hear from a tractor. By 17 months there were no sounds, no eye contact, no smiles. The fact is that our little boy had disappeared. He would line up all of his toy cars and trains in a line and in colour order. He would not lift his head when I called his name and to me he seemed lost and unhappy.

Initially I thought there was a problem with his hearing, but as there had been developmental difficulties with our eldest child we knew that, with Tim, the problems were more deep-rooted and he was diagnosed as having autism.

The reality that Tim had this lifelong incurable disability did not hit home until several months later and – even seven years on – I still find it difficult to comprehend. But this is not about me; this is about finding the right support, interventions and fighting for what he is entitled to. He is currently attending a fantastic special school along with his brother. Both boys are doing remarkably well and the main object is that they are very happy and achieving.'

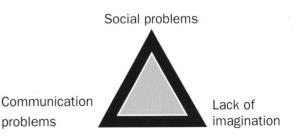

Social problems

Communication problems

Lack of imagination

Autism and inheritance

Genes are like chemical instruction manuals that guide the development of the body and the way it works. They determine things like the colour of your eyes and hair. We get our genes from our parents. Sometimes genes do not work properly – they give the wrong instructions. When this happens, it can cause illnesses, or disabilities, such as autism.

As autism covers such a wide range of conditions, researchers think it is likely that there are a number of genes involved. One faulty gene acting by itself cannot cause autism, but a number acting together might. This makes the search for the genes that trigger autism much more difficult.

The risk to siblings

About three per cent, a little over one in thirty, of the brothers and sisters of children with autism are likely to develop symptoms of autism, too. They are about fifty to a hundred times more likely to develop autism than other children. This would

OF PEAS AND PEOPLE

An Austrian monk called Gregor Mendel (1822-84) first showed that characteristics could be passed from one generation to the next. For many years he studied pea plants and their offspring, showing for example that peas with white flowers would produce offspring that had white flowers, too. He thought that each characteristic was determined by a different inherited unit. We now call these units genes and believe that some characteristics, such as autism, may be caused by a number of genes acting together.

seem to be a clear pointer to the fact that autism runs in families, which means that it is inherited.

Identical twins are identical because they share the same genes. So you would expect that if one twin had an ASD the other twin would, too. This is not necessarily the case. In fact, some studies show that only 60 per cent of identical twins with an ASD both have it. The fact that it is not 100 per cent is further evidence of just how complex a condition autism actually is.

Different for boys

Autism is much more common in boys than it is in girls. The reason for this may be that autism is actually a more extreme version of the 'male brain'. Evidence for this was found recently when scientists at the University of Cambridge discovered that both boys and girls who had been exposed to high levels of testosterone – a hormone that affects brain development and plays a part in puberty in boys – before birth had an increased likelihood of developing autism. The researchers cautioned that the results did not prove that the testosterone was a cause of autism, as both the increased testosterone levels and the symptoms of autism might be caused by another, as yet unknown, factor.

Gene hunt

Scientists who study genes have very sophisticated equipment at their disposal. They can compare the genes of hundreds of people with ASDs and look for similarities between them. Recently, a study of over 1200 families who have members with autism, found that they all had variations in particular genes that are important in controlling the way brain cells work. The challenge now is to develop and test treatments based on these findings.

▼ *Even though identical twins are genetically the same, it does not necessarily mean that if one has autism the other will too.*

The triggers of autism

Researchers have been working hard to find out why one person has an ASD while another person does not. It is likely that there is more than one factor at work, but no one really knows, as yet, what the causes might be.

As we have seen, it is very likely that inheritance has a major part to play. However, the way in which we develop is a result of inherited factors and environmental factors working together. Might there be influences in the environment that act in some way to trigger the development of autism?

At present, researchers have yet to uncover anything in the environment that definitely causes autism, although several ideas have been put forward.

▼ *A doctor prepares to administer the MMR vaccine to a child. Controversial research, since widely rejected, appeared to link its use with the onset of autism.*

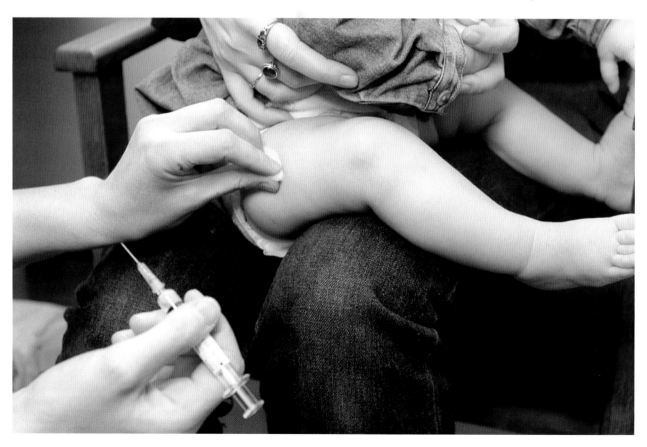

Autism and vaccination

In recent years some controversial research aroused concern among parents that the MMR vaccine could trigger autism. This vaccine is given to children aged between one and two years to protect them from the dangerous illnesses measles, mumps and rubella. Coincidentally, it is also around this time that the first signs of autism may appear. There were cases of autism long before the MMR vaccine was introduced in 1988, and there is no evidence to show that MMR causes autism.

Autism and mercury

Mercury is used as a preservative in many vaccines (but not the MMR vaccine) that are used to give protection from diseases, such as diphtheria and tetanus. There are concerns that exposure to mercury may be one of the triggers for autism. Although it is used in very, very small amounts in vaccines, mercury is in fact a poison. Exposure to mercury has been associated with some psychological disorders, but there is nothing to link it to autism. Vaccines are now increasingly being made without mercury.

Autism and food intolerance

Recent studies have suggested a link between autism and intolerance to some foodstuffs. Some parents have found it helpful to give their child with autism a diet that is free of gluten and casein. Gluten is found in cereal plants, such as wheat and oats, and casein is found in milk. Perhaps the genes involved in dealing with gluten and casein in the body are also involved in autism. You can read more about this on page 23.

DOES TELEVISION CAUSE AUTISM?

In 2006 a study produced statistics to show that in parts of America where cable TV subscriptions were increasing, autism was increasing, too. The study showed that 'approximately 17 per cent of the growth in autism in California and Pennsylvania during the 1970s and 1980s was due to the growth of cable television'. Since the study did not actually measure how much television young children were watching, most autism researchers dismissed its findings.

▲ *In 2006 an idea was put forward that autism could be caused by watching too much television.*

Autism and the body

There has been considerable interest recently in the possibility of a link between autism and disorders of the digestive system. One suggestion is that a digestive disorder may be one of the causes of autism. However, there has so far been little evidence to support this theory.

Researchers have discovered that some children with an ASD have excess quantities of intestinal yeast, a type of micro-organism found in the digestive system. This can lead to the production of chemicals that have an effect on the brain and nervous system, particularly on those parts of the brain that control behaviour and speech. The result of this is that the person may have problems sleeping, lack concentration, be bad tempered and have problems with speech.

▼ *There is some evidence to suggest that diet can have an effect on the symptoms of some people with autism. A link between autism and digestive disorders is an interesting possibility.*

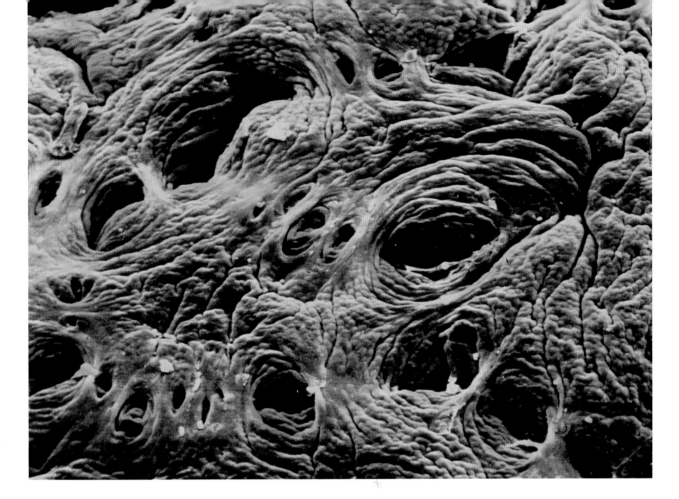

Casein and gluten

On page 21 we saw that that some children with an ASD can be intolerant to certain foodstuffs, such as gluten or casein. These children may show an improvement in their behaviour if they follow a diet that is free of these substances. With some people the change in behaviour becomes apparent in just a few weeks, but with others it may be a year before any difference is noticed. This change in diet does not work for everyone and some children do not show any changes at all. The effects depend on the individual person, another indication that everyone with an ASD is different.

Celiac disease

Celiac disease is a digestive disease that causes damage to the small intestine and interferes with the body's ability to absorb nutrients from food. People with celiac disease cannot tolerate the

▲ *This electron microscope image shows the lining of the small intestine. Normally this would be lined by small projections called villi, but these have been damaged as a result of celiac disease.*

presence of gluten in their food. It was thought that people with autism were more likely than others to have celiac disease, too. However, in 2007 researchers compared 34 children with autism to 34 children without autism. The children were aged between four and sixteen. Their study revealed that children with autism were actually at no greater risk of developing celiac disease than anyone else.

So, although there may very well be a link that remains to be uncovered, the food intolerance suffered by people with ASDs may be caused by something entirely different from the intolerance to gluten shown by people with celiac disease.

Autism and mental health

Autism is a problem with the development of the brain, it is not caused by problems with mental health. However, people with autism can have mental health problems, just like everybody else.

There are obvious difficulties in diagnosing mental health problems in someone with communication difficulties, but it seems apparent that many autistic people can suffer from depression and anxiety and there is also evidence of a link between autism and sleep disorders.

In dealing with a person with an ASD, the psychiatrist has to be aware of the style of communication that is normal for that person. A person with autism may have ways of dealing with others that are peculiar to them, but which have nothing to do with mental health problems.

Asperger syndrome and mental health

People with Asperger syndrome seem to be particularly likely to suffer from mental health issues, especially as they move from adolescence into adulthood. One study found that two-thirds of patients with Asperger syndrome were affected in some way.

Depression is common in people with Asperger syndrome, perhaps triggered by a growing awareness of their condition as they get older. People with autism are also likely to feel anxious. These feelings of anxiety may lead them to retreat into repetitive

behaviour as a way of regaining control over a worrying situation. Sometimes these feelings can be managed by using relaxation techniques or by doing physical activity, such as bouncing on a trampoline or going for a walk.

Autism and bullying

A recent study looked at over 50,000 children aged between six and seventeen. The researchers were interested in finding out whether children with autism were more likely to bully other children. They suspected that children with autism might bully more than others for a variety of reasons. For example, they are more often male, and boys are more likely to be bullies than girls; they may well have been bullied themselves because of their autism, and victims are more likely to become bullies in turn; and many children with autism require treatment for aggression.

What the researchers found was that children with autism were no more likely to be bullies unless they also had the condition known as attention deficit hyperactivity disorder (ADHD). ADHD is a behavioural disorder in which a child has difficulty concentrating, may be hyperactive

and have learning difficulties. Those with both disorders showed a rate of bullying that was four times higher than other children. They also had a higher rate of bullying than children with ADHD but no autism. About half of children with an ASD also suffer from ADHD and so may require additional support to help them deal with this issue.

▲ *Some children with autism may be bullied at school because they are seen to be 'different'. Children with autism who also have ADHD may also be bullies themselves.*

Can autism be treated?

Not surprisingly, one of the first reactions of a parent whose child has been diagnosed as having an ASD is to ask what can be done about it. Autism is a lifelong condition that cannot be cured with medication at the moment. However, there are things that can be done to make life easier for people with ASDs and their families.

Applied behaviour analysis

Applied behaviour analysis (ABA) is a form of behavioural therapy that seems to have benefits for many people with ASDs. It works by teaching the child 'to learn how to learn'. Children with autism might find it difficult to cope with complex information, so social and other skills are broken down into small steps making each one easy to grasp. As the child successfully accomplishes each step he or she is rewarded, while undesired behaviour is either ignored or redirected. Gradually the child can learn how to communicate with others and how to act in different situations.

ABA is carried out on a one-to-one basis with a qualified therapist in a controlled environment. Very gradually the therapist brings 'distractions' into the sessions, slowly getting the child used to dealing with a more natural setting. It takes a great deal of effort, and the therapist works with the child over about 30 to 40 hours a week. In the most intense form of ABA, the therapist will be with the child for eight hours a day over a two-year period. However, because of this huge commitment in time, ABA can be a very expensive form of treatment and so may not be available to everyone.

◄ *Over time, a trained therapist, working one-to-one with a child with autism, can help that child to cope with the world around them.*

▲ *Many people with autism readily take to using computers as they can focus directly on what is happening on the screen and ignore any distractions.*

Medicine

Sometimes medication can be prescribed to reduce some of the specific symptoms of autism. For example, some medicines can be used to help relieve agitation and anxiety, and to deal with obsessional or hyperactive behaviour. The drawback is that, as with many drugs, there can be harmful side effects if they are used over a long period. For example, a drug that helps to reduce hyperactivity can result in an increase in repetitive behaviour.

Computers and autism

Computers have long been recognised as a valuable aid in teaching people with an ASD. Many people with autism seem to find it very comfortable to use a computer. When they are focusing on the narrow area of the computer screen they can ignore distractions around them more easily. Using a computer can help people with autism to gain an awareness of themselves and their actions as, simply by touching a key on the keyboard, they can see an immediate change on the computer screen. Through the use of games, computers can also help people with autism to learn how to interact with others.

THE VALUE OF COMPUTERS

For a person with autism computers are valuable because:

· they provide a controlled, predictable environment

· they allow errors to be made safely

· they can be used to express ideas verbally and non-verbally

· they can be programmed to suit different requirements.

Living with autism

What is daily life like for people with autism? How do they see themselves and others, and how do they cope with the 'confusing mass of events, people, sounds and sights', as one person with autism described reality?

Many people with an ASD have difficulty understanding their feelings and relating to the feelings of others. They may experience difficulties managing emotions, such as stress, anxiety and frustration, and this can sometimes lead to outbursts of anger or aggression. Of course, these things do not just apply to people with autism. Having problems with your feelings can simply be a part of being human!

DR TEMPLE GRANDIN

Dr Temple Grandin is a very accomplished and well-known adult with autism. Until she was three and a half Dr Grandin did not speak but relied upon sounds, such as humming and screaming, to communicate. She was greatly helped with many hours of therapy to learn speech and social skills. Today Dr Grandin is a successful livestock handling equipment designer, an award-winning author and a speaker on the subject of autism. She says, 'To [some] people, it is incomprehensible that the characteristics of autism can be modified and controlled. However, I feel strongly that I am living proof that they can.'

▲ *Music therapy can work very well for some children with autism, perhaps because it offers them a non-verbal means of expressing themselves.*

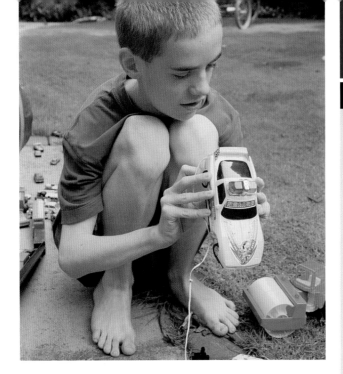

▲ *A child with autism may seem to inhabit their own world, where the needs of others play little part.*

Challenging behaviour

People with autism say that their world is actually a very logical one. What may be seen as 'challenging behaviour' to someone else probably makes perfect sense to the person with autism. This confusion arises from the different ways in which people with an ASD try to make sense of the world. They may be frustrated by their inability to communicate their needs, or be made anxious by changes in routine that seem trivial to a person who does not have autism.

Children with autism may develop strategies for getting what they want that seem unacceptable to others. For example, children who want to have some quiet time on their own may recall that when they pulled someone's hair on a previous occasion they were sent out of the room. So when they want to be on their own they pull the other child's hair again. Once the reason for the behaviour is understood, alternative signals can be arranged with a parent or teacher. For example, children could pick up a red ball as a signal to their teacher that they would like some quiet time on their own.

CASE NOTES

NATASHA'S 'HEADACHES'

Natasha is 14 and has severe autism. Her speech consists of single words and set phrases. She is able to communicate basic needs through words, symbols and signing. Natasha is very attached to her mother who serves as a model for many of her behaviours.

Natasha's mother suffers from severe headaches. Sometimes, when Natasha appears upset and is challenging at home, her mother uses this as a possible 'explanation' of her behaviour. She asks Natasha 'What's wrong?' and then (when Natasha does not respond) asks 'Do you have a headache?' Natasha has learnt to say 'Yes' to this, as it leads to more attention from her mother.

However, an unwanted consequence of this pattern arose recently when Natasha went away on a school trip. After two days away, Natasha began to show signs of being very unwell. Staff wondered whether she was homesick, but on the third day Natasha vomited, had an elevated temperature and was showing clear signs of distress. An inexperienced member of staff asked Natasha what was wrong. Natasha confidently answered that she had a headache.

The senior member of staff was more aware of Natasha's history and of the unreliability of her responses to questions, and Natasha was taken to hospital. There it was discovered she had acute appendicitis which would have proved fatal had it been left longer.

Autism and families

Life can be challenging for the siblings and parents of a person with an ASD. How do other members of the family cope when they discover that a child in the family has an ASD?

Diagnosis

It can be hard for parents to admit that there is something 'wrong' with their child, particularly if the difference is not visible to others. The earlier a diagnosis is made, the better the chance of a person with an ASD and their family getting the support they need quickly and effectively. Diagnosis can bring these benefits for the family:

• a sense of relief and understanding that they are not 'unusual'

• access to services and help that they might not realise they are entitled to

• a better understanding of how they can deal with the particular needs of the family member with an ASD

• the chance to explore the range of therapies available to help the person with an ASD to cope with their condition.

▼ *A doctor tests a boy for autism; in this case by watching how he reacts to different facial expressions. People with autism have difficulty in understanding how others are feeling.*

Sisters and brothers

Having a brother or sister with autism can be particularly confusing for other children in the family. They may realise that there is something different about their sibling, but not be able to understand what it is, particularly if they are younger. This might make them feel angry, jealous, sad and frustrated, perhaps if they see their brother or sister getting more attention from their parents, or not being told off for 'bad behaviour'.

For these reasons, it is of vital importance that other children in the family have the situation explained to them as clearly as possible and are encouraged to share their feelings and learn how they can help their sibling and their parents.

▼ *If one child in a family has autism the chances of his or her siblings also having it are increased. All three of these brothers have some degree of autism.*

A SISTER'S VIEW

I was 12 years old when I realised I was embarrassed by my sister's behaviour. My mum, sister and I went to Woolworths and my sister's behaviour was very erratic and aggressive. She knocked off a mug from one of the shelves and instead of going to help or pick up the broken pieces I walked away. I was ashamed of my sister. I will never forget the car journey home, and the look that my mum gave me. I may have been embarrassed by my sister's actions, but she was embarrassed by mine. I knew that I was wrong to be feeling this way, but I couldn't help it. I just could not understand why everyone else's brothers and sisters were 'normal' and mine wasn't.

Autism and school

Sympathetic education and support can go a long way towards making life better for people with ASDs. Provisions for education have to be varied and adaptable because the range of needs across the autistic spectrum is so wide.

How a child with autism copes with school will be affected by the severity of the autism. While those on the mid to lower range of the autistic spectrum will need the support offered by specialist schools, others in the higher ranges may adapt to life in mainstream schools, learning alongside children without autism. It will be up to the parents or carers to decide what is best for their child.

Pre-school education

Starting to learn early is essential for a child with an ASD. There is a great deal of evidence that shows that the earlier help is given, the more likely the child is to adapt to his or her condition. Many parents have found that placing their child in a nursery school that is sympathetic to his or her requirements can have great benefits in developing the child's social skills and communication with others.

Going to school

Going to school is a big challenge for children with autism. They will not be used to being in a place that they do not know, where there are so many other people to deal with and new routines to get used to.

▼ *With a great deal of patience and understanding, it is possible to help a child with autism learn how to use speech to communicate their needs.*

ALEXANDER'S STORY

Alexander is 11 and was diagnosed with Asperger syndrome when he was nine. He attends a mainstream primary school with a minimum of help and is very bright academically, but he has some motor skills difficulties as well as social skills problems. He is very sensitive to noise and dislikes crowds, but has learned to cope. He only had one good friend at school, who moved away two years ago.

'I'm in year 6. I enjoy mental arithmetic, literacy and science. Partly, 'cos I'm good at it, but partly because I'm beating everyone in the class. Well, almost everyone. When I beat people it's exhilarating. There are about 29 people in my class because there are usually one or two off sick, 31 in total. It feels a bit full at times...it makes me feel claustrophobic, but I try and act as normal. I virtually always succeed. For some reason I think it makes my body temperature go up. I go to the library at break time – it's quiet and there aren't many people. It feels a lot better. I like the books, they are better company when everyone's screaming around outside.

'I eat lunch in the hall. I feel claustrophobic. It's deafeningly loud, 'cos everyone's always screaming. The teachers have to hit the tables, a metal table with a metal spoon, to get everyone to shut up. They did it yesterday. [The kids] started shouting but a bit less loudly after the teacher had finished speaking. Sometimes people come and help me in class. They take me out and talk about things that happened recently. They tell me what I'm supposed to be doing. It's difficult to understand sometimes. Everyone has a timetable on the interactive whiteboard. It helps being able to see what's going on.'

To help with these problems, it is a good idea for the child to have the opportunity to visit the school first and have the chance to meet the teachers. Parents can then talk through any anxieties and problems the child may have before the big day of joining the new school actually arrives.

Further education

There are currently only a few further education courses that have been designed specifically with people with an ASD in mind. However, the law requires that further education centres do not discriminate against or exclude people who require additional support, which includes people with ASDs. The college or university must make reasonable adjustments to ensure that no student is unduly disadvantaged. These adjustments include making the surroundings safe and accessible and providing aids and services as required by the students.

Asperger syndrome

Asperger syndrome may be considered to be the mildest form of autism. People with Asperger syndrome are often of average and above average intelligence, for example there are people with Asperger syndrome working successfully as computer programmers and university professors.

More than any other type of person with an ASD, people with Asperger syndrome can learn to lead full and independent lives. Dr Lorna Wing (see pages 16-17) described the main features of Asperger syndrome as:

- Lack of empathy

- Naive, inappropriate, one-sided interaction

- Little or no ability to form friendships

- Pedantic, repetitive speech

- Poor non-verbal communication

- Intense absorption in certain subjects

- Clumsy and ill-co-ordinated movements and odd postures

Asperger syndrome and language

People with Asperger syndrome tend to have fewer difficulties with language than people on the lower end of the autistic spectrum, but their speech patterns may seem 'strange'. Although they can have excellent vocabularies, their speech may be stilted and repetitive. One person with Asperger syndrome described ordinary conversation as 'like trying to understand a foreign language'. A person with Asperger syndrome may also take things literally, which may

BORN TO THRIVE

Joshua Muggleton is 18 and has Asperger syndrome. Since the age of 15, Joshua has led workshops and given talks on autism and autistic spectrum disorders, and related issues. Joshua's interactive workshops and lectures have grown in popularity and he regularly talks to teachers, parents and professionals on life with Asperger syndrome. He has even given a speech in the House of Commons. He says:

'We are not born to suffer. We are born to thrive. If you live in a dry area and your garden receives little water, you plant plants which like dry soil. But when you are given a plant that likes wet soil, you don't kill it, you water it, you spend one of your 1440 minutes each day watering that plant. Because you know, that given the right care, that little bit of effort can produce spectacular blooms. And so it should be with children like us.'

lead to misunderstandings. For example, if they are told that a DVD is 'really cool' they might expect it to be cold to the touch, rather than really good.

▼ *Orion Academy in California has been specially designed to meet the needs of children with Asperger syndrome and high-functioning autism.*

Living with Asperger syndrome

People with Asperger syndrome often have low self-esteem. This may be the result of being misunderstood and rejected by those around them. They can find it hard to make friends, even though they may very much want to, because they lack the social and language skills that others take for granted.

Autism and adulthood

It is all too easy to think of autism as being something that affects children, but no one 'grows out' of autism. It is a condition that lasts for life and the challenges faced by the child with autism will also have to be faced as an adult.

Some people with autism will need supervision and support all through their lives. Adults with low-functioning autism will require the constant care and attention that they needed as children. They will have to be taken care of by their families or in residential care homes. Adults with high-functioning autism and people with Asperger syndrome on the other hand, can do very well. However, there is a range of opportunities available for people with ASDs.

Working with autism

It is estimated that about a third of people with autism can live and work with some degree of independence. How far this is possible depends to a large extent on the wider community's willingness to be understanding and supportive of their needs. An important consideration is to play to the person with autism's strengths. For example, they may be excellent at performing complex repetitive tasks that involve good hand and eye co-ordination, such as laboratory work or assembling electronics components.

Diagnosing autism in adults

There are doubtless many people at the high end of the autistic spectrum who go through childhood and into adult life without ever realising that they have an ASD. Sometimes a person will read an article on autism and recognise something of themselves in the description.

◀ *Jay Jensen has high-functioning autism. He has a responsible job doing data entry for the city manager's office in the city of Lodi, California, USA.*

Some people who suspect that they may have an ASD in adulthood will want to have this confirmed by a proper diagnosis. To do this they will have to visit their doctor and ask to be referred to a psychiatrist or psychologist with experience in diagnosing autism. Having their condition diagnosed can result in a number of benefits, such as reaching a greater understanding of themselves and being able to get help to deal with their needs.

AUTISM ALERT

The National Autistic Society in Britain has developed the Autism Alert card to be carried by people with ASDs. It can help them to let other people know of their needs in situations where communication may be difficult, for example in a busy railway station. The card holds emergency contact details and a leaflet explaining key facts about autism.

▲ *People with autism can carry alert cards such as this that hold valuable information explaining their condition to others.*

DAVID'S STORY

David is 25 years old and has autism. He uses just a few signs to communicate that only people who know him well can understand. If he is touched, even accidentally, by another person, he becomes very anxious and needs to perform repetitive rituals, sometimes for a couple of hours. If he is interrupted while doing this it can result in a full-blown panic attack, during which he may lose control and become aggressive.

This can be prevented if people around David understand his needs. He needs to be given a lot of time to absorb new information and to prepare for change. He may take up to five full minutes to digest what he is told, but when he has done so he will indicate his understanding by nodding. This indicates that he is ready for the next piece of information or the activity. This kind of communication requires patience – if David's thought process is interrupted by further information being given too soon, then he may become 'stuck' at that point and unable to move on. However, if he is allowed to take the time he needs, he is able to control his anxieties.

The future for autism

What does the future hold for autism? Is a cure, or prevention, even remotely possible? Should we not, as some people believe, even be looking for a cure, but accept people with ASDs as they are?

Research continues into trying to uncover the genetic causes of autism, and it may be in this area that the greatest hope for therapy or prevention is to be found. It is a complicated picture. At the moment researchers believe that there may be as many as thirty genes involved in autism. Alterations to these genes may be what leads to the condition of autism. The greater the number of altered genes, the more likely the person is to show the symptoms of autism.

▼ *Genetics laboratories across the world are involved in the search for the causes of autism.*

THE AUTISTIC LIBERATION FRONT

Many people with autism do not want to be changed. They object to people who describe them as 'suffering' from Asperger syndrome, for example. They say that this is just the way they are, they have no disease and so they require no cure. In the USA, people with autism sell Autistic Liberation Front badges and campaign for the 'dignity of autistic citizens'.

Fragile X

Scientists in the USA have genetically modified mice so that they show symptoms of Fragile X Syndrome. Fragile X Syndrome is linked to a mutation in a particular gene. This gene produces an enzyme that affects the development of the connections between brain cells. It is a condition that is believed to cause a range of symptoms, from learning difficulties to autism, in humans. The genetically modified mice with the condition appeared to wander around aimlessly and keep making the same movements.

Next the scientists blocked the activity of the enzyme produced by the Fragile X gene. They found that doing this reversed the symptoms of the condition. The mice stopped behaving oddly. They also found that the connections between brain cells in the mice had returned to normal.

▲ *This four-year-old boy has Fragile X syndrome, a condition that may have links to autism.*

The researchers were keen to point out that the treatment was not begun until several weeks after the symptoms of Fragile X had first appeared. This was exciting because it meant that treatments could potentially be developed for children who had suffered from the symptoms of Fragile X for a long time.

Help for today

As well as looking to the future, and the possibility of preventing autism, a great deal of research is being focused on helping people with autism today. This involves doing as much as possible to understand them and their needs, and encouraging the rest of society to accept them as people in their own right.

Glossary

ADHD (Attention Deficit Hyperactivity Disorder) a disorder in which a child cannot keep their attention on anything and may be restless and overactive

abnormality a health problem or feature that is not normally present in a healthy individual

adolescence the period of change from childhood to adulthood during which puberty is taking place

Asperger syndrome a form of autism where a person may have difficulty with communication, social interaction and understanding others' thoughts and feelings

autistic spectrum a wide range of conditions by which people show symptoms of autism to varying degrees of severity

Autistic spectrum disorder (ASD) a condition that appears on the autistic spectrum. People with ASDs tend to show the same symptoms, but with varying degrees of severity

biological to do with life and living things

casein a substance found in milk and some cheeses

diagnose to identify a disease or condition after careful examination of the body and symptoms

diptheria a disease that causes difficulty breathing and swallowing

electron microscope a very powerful microscope

empathy the ability to understand and share the feelings of others

environment the influences and conditions that surround us and have an effect on us

enzyme a chemical that controls the speed of a chemical reaction in the body

factor something that helps to cause a result

Fragile X syndrome a disorder that is caused by a mutation in a particular gene. It can have many symptoms from learning difficulties to autism, attention disorders or hyperactivity

gene the basic unit of heredity by which characteristics are passed from one generation to the next

gluten a substance found in cereals, such as oats and wheat

high-functioning a person at the top end of the autistic spectrum might be said to have high-functioning autism, they are more capable, and their symptoms are less severe, than those at the low end of the spectrum

hormone a chemical made by one part of your body that causes a change or reaction in another part of your body

impairment a weakness or damage

inheritance the process of passing on physical characteristics from parents to their offspring

low-functioning a person at the low end of the autistic spectrum might be said to have low-functioning autism, they are less capable, and their symptoms are more severe, than those at the high end of the spectrum

MMR a vaccination given to children to protect them from the dangerous illnesses measles, mumps and rubella

motor skills ability to do tasks that use muscles, such as throwing a ball or writing

mutation a change that takes place in a gene that may result in children having different characteristics from their parents

naive lacking experience or judgement

nutrients substances that are necessary for growth and health

obsessional being continually preoccupied with a particular thought or action to a troubling degree

pedantic very concerned with minor details

psychiatrist a doctor who specialises in diagnosing and treating mental disorders

psychologist a person involved in the scientific study of the mind and mental processes

radiation energy that is transmitted in the form of waves or particles

researcher a person who investigates and studies in order to establish facts

rubella a disease that is a mild form of measles, and is also known as German measles

siblings brothers and sisters

side effects the effects that a drug or treatment might have in addition to the desired effects it has – side effects may be harmful and undesirable

social skills the ability to talk to, and engage in activities with, other people

spectrum a scale extending between two extremes

stereotyped an action that is similar every time it is carried out

symbolic using a symbol or an object to stand for an idea

symptoms changes in the body that can indicate that a disease or other condition is present

testosterone a hormone that tells the body to produce or enhance male characteristics, it is present in males and females

tetanus a disease that causes muscle stiffness and spasms

therapy measures that are taken to treat a disease or condition

triad a set of three things that are connected to each other in some way

vaccine/vaccination something that helps the body prepare for an infection by a disease-causing virus; giving a vaccine is called vaccination

Further information

Books

Fiction

A Wizard Alone, Young Wizards,
Diane Duane, *Magic Carpet Books, 2003*

Are You Alone on Purpose?
Nancy Werlin, *Speak, 2007*

My Brother Kevin has Autism,
Richard W Carlson, *Writers Club Press, 2001*

Running on Dreams,
Herb Heiman, *Autism Asperger Publishing Company, 2007*

The Curious Incident of the Dog in the Night-time,
Mark Haddon, *Vintage, 2004*

Non-Fiction

Asperger syndrome: an Owner's manual: What you, your parents and your teachers need to know,
Ellen Korin, *Autism Asperger Publishing Company, 2006*

Autism and Asperger syndrome,
Ana Maria Rodriguez, *Twenty First Century Medical Library, 2008*

Autism (Health Issues),
Sarah Lennard-Brown, *Hodder Wayland, 2006*

Autism (Perspectives on Diseases and Disorders),
Carrie Fredericks, *Greenhaven Press, 2007*

**Can I Tell You About Asperger Syndrome?
A Guide for Friends and Family,**
Jude Welton, *Jessica Kingsley Publishers, 2003*

Coping with Asperger syndrome,
Maxine Rosaler, *Rosen Publishing Group, 2005*

**Freaks, Geeks and Asperger Syndrome:
A User Guide to Adolescence,**
Luke Jackson, *Jessica Kingsley Publishers, 2002*

I'm Not Naughty – I'm Autistic: Jodi's Journey,
Jean Shaw, *Jessica Kingsley Publishers, 2002*

**Ten Things Every Child With Autism
Wishes You Knew,**
Ellen Notbohm, *Future Horizons Inc., 2007*

Thomas Has Autism (Like Me, Like You),
Jillian Powell, *Evans Brothers Ltd, 2006*

Understanding Autism for Dummies,
Temple Grandin, Stephen Shore and
Linda G Rastelli, *John Wiley and Sons, 2006*

Films

After Thomas
2 Entertainment Video, 2006
A true story of a couple's struggle to understand the needs of their son who has autism.

Rain Man
MGM Entertainment, 1989, (DVD 2004)
Charlie Babbit discovers he has an older brother, Raymond, who has autism.

Websites

www.aspect.org.au
This Australian website provides information, education and other services through partnership with people with autistic spectrum disorders, their families and communities.

www.autisminfo.org.au
Autism Info Australia provide clear information for parents on what ASD means and outline some of the services and treatments available today in Australia. They also work towards promoting services on a local, state and national level including support groups, state bodies, local projects and more.

www.autismresearchcentre.com/arc/default.asp
The Autism Research Centre, based at Cambridge University, aims to understand the causes of autism and to develop new ways of assessing and helping those with an autistic spectrum disorder.

www.autism-society.org/site/PageServer
The Autism Society of America website has information for people affected by autism, those on the spectrum, family members and professionals.

http://autismsocietycanada.ca/index_e.html
Autism Society Canada (ASC) is a national charitable organization. It was founded in 1976 by a group of parents committed to public education, information and referral, and support for its regional societies.

www.autismspeaks.org/
Autism Speaks is 'dedicated to funding global biomedical research into the causes, prevention, treatments and cure for autism'.

www.autismuk.com
This website provides links to autism organisations around the world.

www.cdc.gov/ncbddd/autism/
Information on current research into autism from the US Centers for Disease Control and Prevention website.

www.kidshealth.org/kid/health_problems/brain/autism.html
An easy to understand introduction to autism and the problems it brings - part of the Kids Health website.

www.nas.org.uk/
The National Autistic Society - championing the rights and interests of people with autism and their families in the UK.

Note to parents and teachers: Every effort has been made by the Publishers to ensure that these websites are suitable for children, that they are of the highest educational value, and that they contain no inappropriate or offensive material. However, because of the nature of the Internet, it is impossible to guarantee that the contents of these sites will not be altered. We strongly advise that Internet access is supervised by a responsible adult.

Index

ADHD 24-25
anxiety 24, 27, 28
Applied behaviour analysis (ABA) 26
Asperger, Hans 11, 15
Asperger syndrome 11, 14-15, 24, 33, 34-35, 36, 38
Autism alert card 37
Autistic Liberation Front 38
autistic spectrum 9, 14-15, 32, 33, 34, 36
autistic spectrum disorder (ASD):
    ADHD 24-25
    Asperger syndrome 34-35
    autistic spectrum 14-15
    diagnosing 16
    digestive problems 22-23
    education 32-33
    future 38
    inheritance 18-19
    living with 28-29, 30-31, 36-37
    mental health 24-25
    rise in 12-13
    treatment 26-27
    triggers 20

brain 8, 13, 19, 22, 24, 39
bullying 24, 25

casein 21, 23
causes 11, 13, 16, 18-19, 20-21, 22-23, 24, 38-39
celiac disease 23
Checklist for autism in toddlers (CHAT) 16
Childhood disintegrative disorder (CDD) 15
communication problems 8, 15, 16-17, 24, 26, 28-29, 32, 34, 37
computers 27, 34
cure 26, 38

depression 24

diagnosis 9, 12-13, 16-17, 24, 26, 30, 36-37
digestive system 22
disease 8, 11, 21, 23, 38

education 32, 33
environmental factors 11, 13, 20

family 9, 30-31
food intolerance 21, 23
Fragile X syndrome 39
friendships 11, 17, 34-35
further education 33

genes 18, 19, 21, 38-39
gluten 21, 23
Grandin, Dr Temple 28

high-functioning autism 9, 14-15, 32, 35, 36

imagination 17
increase in autism 12, 13
Itard, Jean 11

Kanner, Leo 11, 15
Kanner syndrome 14, 15

learning difficulties 9, 12, 25, 39
low-functioning autism 9, 14, 15, 34, 36

'male brain' 19
Mendel, Gregor 18
mental health 24-25
mercury 21
MMR 20, 21
mobile phones 13
music therapy 28

parents 9, 11, 16, 18, 21, 30, 31, 32, 34
pesticides 13
plastic bottles 13

pollution 13
pre-school education 32
processed food 13
psychiatrist 24, 37
psychologist 37

'refrigerator mothers' 11
relationships 8
Rett syndrome 15

rise of autism 12-13

school 17, 25, 29, 32-33
siblings 18, 30, 31
sleep disorders 24
social problems 16-17
social skills 11, 15, 26, 28, 32, 33, 35
symptoms 11, 12, 13, 15, 18, 19, 22, 27, 38, 39

Taylor, Brent 13
television 21
testosterone 19
triad of impairments 16, 17
trigger 18, 20-21, 24
twins 19

United States of America (USA) 8, 12, 36, 38, 39

vaccinations 13, 21
vaccine 20, 21

wild boy of Aveyron, the 11
Wing, Dr Lorna 16, 17, 34
working 34, 36

These are the list of contents for each title in Explaining:

Asthma
What is asthma? • History of asthma • Increase in asthma • Who has asthma? • Healthy lungs • How asthma affects the lungs • What triggers asthma? • Asthma and allergies • Diagnosing asthma • Preventing an attack • Relieving an attack • What to do during an attack • Growing up with asthma • Living with asthma • Asthma and exercise • Future

Autism
What is autism? • Autism: a brief history • The rise of autism • The autistic spectrum • The signs of autism • Autism and inheritance • The triggers of autism • Autism and the body • Autism and mental health • Can autism be treated? • Living with autism • Autism and families • Autism and school • Asperger syndrome • Autism and adulthood • The future for autism

Blindness
What is blindness? • Causes and effects • Visual impairment • Colour blindness and night blindness • Eye tests • Treatments and cures • Coping with blindness • Optical aids • Guide dogs and canes • Home life • On the move • Blindness and families • Blindness at school • Blindness as an adult • Blindness, sport and leisure • The future for blindness

Cerebral Palsy
What is cerebral palsy? • The causes of cerebral palsy • Diagnosis • Types of cerebral palsy • Other effects of cerebral palsy • Managing cerebral palsy • Other support • Technological support • Communication • How it feels • Everyday life • Being at school • Cerebral palsy and the family • Into adulthood • Raising awareness • The future

Cystic Fibrosis
What is cystic fibrosis? • A brief history • What causes cystic fibrosis? • Screening and diagnosis • The effects of cystic fibrosis • How is cystic fibrosis managed? • Infections and illness • A special diet • Clearing the airways • Physical exercise • Cystic fibrosis and families • Cystic fibrosis at school • Living with cystic fibrosis • Living longer • New treatments • Gene therapy

Deafness
What is deafness? • Ears and sounds • Types of deafness • Causes of deafness • Signs of deafness • Diagnosis • Treating deafness • Lip reading • Sign language • Deafness and education • Schools for the deaf • Deafness and adulthood • Technology • Deafness and the family • Fighting discrimination • Latest research

Diabetes
What is diabetes? • Type 1 diabetes • Type 2 diabetes • Symptoms and diagnosis • Medication • Hypoglycaemia • Eyes, skin and feet • Other health issues • Healthy eating and drinking • Physical activity • Living with diabetes • Diabetes and families • Diabetes at school • Growing up with diabetes • The future for diabetics

Down's syndrome
What is Down's syndrome? • Changing attitudes • Who has Down's Syndrome? • What are chromosomes? • The extra chromosome • Individual differences • Health problems • Testing for Down's Syndrome • Diagnosing at birth • Babies • Toddlers • At school • Friendships and fun • Effects on the family • Living independently • Down's syndrome community

Epilepsy
What is epilepsy? • Causes and effects • Who has epilepsy? • Partial seizures • Generalised seizures • Triggers • Diagnosis • How you can help • Controlling epilepsy • Taking medicines • Living with epilepsy • Epilepsy and families • Epilepsy at school • Sport and leisure • Growing up with epilepsy • The future for epilepsy

Food allergy
What are food allergies? • Food allergies: a brief history • Food aversion, intolerance or allergy? • What is an allergic reaction? • Food allergies: common culprits • Anaphylaxis • Testing for food allergies • Avoiding allergic reactions • Treating allergic reactions • How common are food allergies? • Food allergies and families • Food allergies and age • Living with food allergies • 21st century problems • The future for food allergies